GEOGRAPHY OF THE WORLD

THE MAGNIFICENT

HIMALAYAS

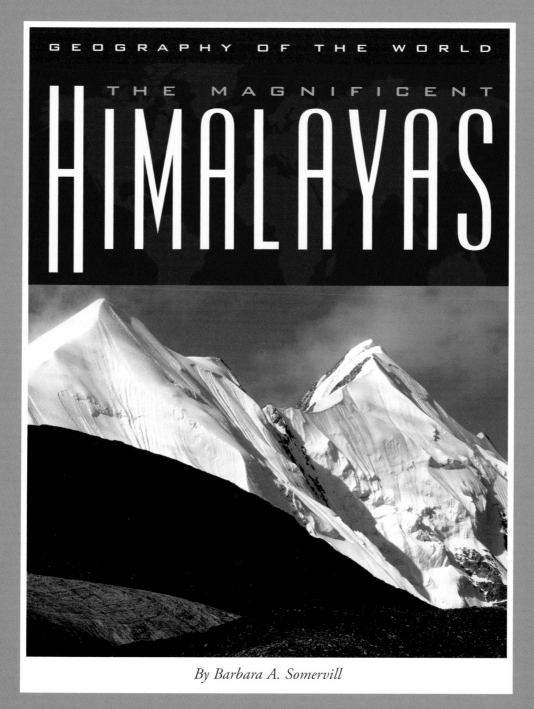

By Barbara A. Somervill

THE CHILD'S WORLD®
CHANHASSEN, MINNESOTA

The Child's World

Published in the United States of America by The Child's World®
PO Box 326, Chanhassen, MN 55317-0326
800-599-READ
www.childsworld.com

Content Adviser:
Mark Williams,
Associate Professor,
University of Colorado,
Boulder, Colorado

Photo Credits: Cover/frontispiece: Craig Lovell/Corbis.
Interior: Animals Animals/Earth Scenes: 6 (OSF/C. Monteath), 17 (Robert Maier);
Corbis: 4 (Bob Winsett), 5 (Robert Holmes), 15 (Roger Wood), 26 (Ric Ergenbright);
Steve McCurry/Magnum Photos: 9, 21; OSF/M. Colbeck/Animals Animals/Earth
Scenes: 12, 14, 18; Galen Rowell/Corbis: 19, 24; Travelsite/Colasanti/Picture Desk:
11, 23.

The Child's World®: Mary Berendes, Publishing Director

Editorial Directions, Inc.: E. Russell Primm, Editorial Director; Melissa McDaniel,
Line Editor; Katie Marsico, Associate Editor; Judi Shiffer, Associate Editor and Library
Media Specialist; Matthew Messbarger, Editorial Assistant; Susan Hindman, Copy
Editor; Sarah E. De Capua and Lucia Raatma, Proofreaders; Marsha Bonnoit, Peter
Garnham, Terry Johnson, Olivia Nellums, Chris Simms, Katherine Trickle, and
Stephen Carl Wender, Fact Checkers; Tim Griffin/IndexServ, Indexer; Cian Loughlin
O'Day, Photo Researcher; Linda S. Koutris, Photo Selector; XNR Productions, Inc.,
Cartographer

The Design Lab: Kathleen Petelinsek, Design and Page Production

Library of Congress Cataloging-in-Publication Data
Somervill, Barbara A.
  The magnificent Himalayas / by Barbara A. Somervill.
     p. cm. — (Geography of the world series)
  Includes index.
  ISBN 1-59296-332-3 (alk. paper)
  1. Himalaya Mountains—Juvenile literature. I. Title. II. Series.
  DS485.H6S66 2004
  915.496—dc22   2004003725

TABLE OF CONTENTS

CHAPTER ONE

FOR VILLAGE PRIDE

One village challenges another. Which one has better archers? The night before the tournament, each village celebrates. Villagers dance and sing. They consult a fortune-teller to discover which team has the winning edge.

Dancers whirl in traditional costumes at this festival in Bhutan.

Archery is the national pastime of Bhutan.

The day of the contest dawns bright and cold. Archers gather on the field. The targets are set at 130 yards (119 meters). Now comes the real test. Which archer has the truest eye, the steadiest aim, the greatest skill? The winner holds the pride of his village in his hands.

No, this is not a story of Robin Hood in "merry old England." This is modern-day Bhutan. Archery is Bhutan's national sport. Yearly tournaments are important events in this country located high in the Himalayas.

CHAPTER TWO

THE MAKING OF A MOUNTAIN RANGE

Mountain building takes millions of years. Yet sometimes the earth is in a hurry and produces mountains rather quickly, at least quickly for **geologic time.**

Mountains are made in several different ways. Volcanoes, earthquakes, incredible pressure, and massive collisions all build mountains.

The continents and ocean floor make up the outer layer of earth,

Nepalese villages lie in the shadows of the world's highest mountain range.

called the crust. The crust is like a broken eggshell. It has cracks and cuts. The different pieces of the broken eggshell are called plates. Earth has about 20 different plates. These plates are constantly moving. About 70 million years ago, the Indian Plate was rushing northward like a speed demon. It crashed full speed into the Asian Plate about 50 million years ago and built the Himalayas.

THE HINDU KUSH
One of the most famous mountain ranges in the Himalayas is called the Hindu Kush. Its name means "Hindu killer." The Hindu Kush is located in what are now Afghanistan and Pakistan. The region holds a special place in history. Long ago, caravans laden with silk and spices traveled from China to Europe through the Hindu Kush. Today, the pass through the mountains has a highway for cars and trucks and a second road for traditional camel caravans.

The Himalayas increase in height from .25 to 4 inches (.6 to 10 centimeters) per year. But not every peak in the mountain range grows the same amount. Instead, the growth is uneven. The peaks are still rising because the Indian Plate is still pushing against the Asian Plate.

Mountains support a variety of **ecosystems.** In the Himalayas, the environment on the southern slopes is very different from that of the northern slopes.

The western and southern foothills of the Himalayas are **tropical.** These foothills were once covered with jungles, but much of the land has been cleared for agriculture. Dense growths of orchids, bamboo, and sal trees fill the uncleared land.

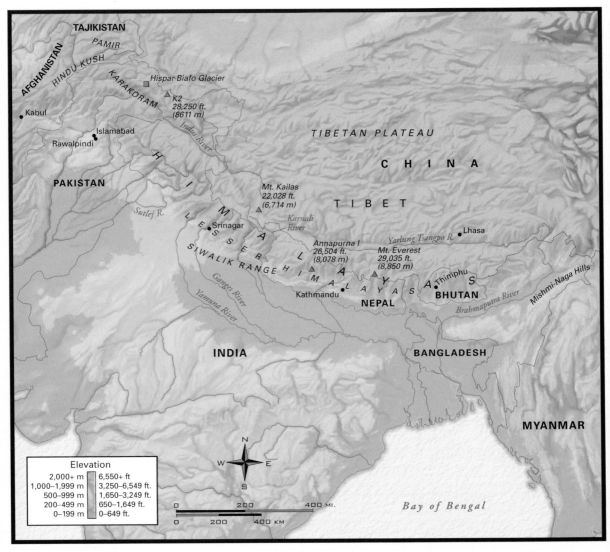

A map of the Himalayas

Moving up the mountains, cedar and pine forests dominate the landscape. In the Himalayas, forests cover the slopes up to between 13,000 and 14,700 feet (3,962 and 4,480 m). Above that height, no trees grow. This is called

Dense forests rise up to the timberline on Himalayan slopes.

the timberline. Around the timberline, rhododendron bushes grow as tall as trees. Still higher is the **tundra,** a treeless region where mosses, lichens, and sedges grow.

Near the peaks of the Himalayas, **glaciers** may cover the ground. The word *Himalaya* means "home of snow." With so many snow-covered peaks and large glaciers, the name is perfect. The Hispar-Biafo Glacier in the mountains of Pakistan is the world's largest glacier outside earth's polar regions. It stretches for more than 76 miles (122 kilometers).

Scientists study the rocks that make up a mountain to learn how the mountain was formed. The Himalayas were once flat seafloor. Sand, clay, and the skeletons of sea creatures collected at the bottom of the sea. Water and gravity put tremendous pressure on this material. In time, it became **sedimentary** rock, such as sandstone or limestone. When the colliding plates folded the land, the sedimentary rock became a mountain. A look inside such a mountain would show the rock in uneven layers, called **strata.**

Pressure and heat can change one type of rock into another. For example, limestone under intense pressure and heat forms marble. Such rocks are called **metamorphic.** The Himalayas are mostly a mix of sedimentary and metamorphic rocks.

CHAPTER THREE

ABOUT THE HIMALAYAS

The Himalayas run east to west. The eastern limit is at Mishmi-Naga in the Burmese mountain chain. The western limit is at Kabul, Afghanistan. In all, the Himalayas are about 1,550 miles (2,500 km) long and 125 to 250 miles (200 to 400 km) wide. The range covers all or parts of Nepal, Bhutan, India, Pakistan, Afghanistan, Tajikistan, and Tibet.

This region of the Karakoram Range in India is bleak and treeless.

Mount Everest presents a challenge for eager mountain climbers.

Several separate mountain ranges make up the Himalayas. The Pamir Range rises in Tajikistan. Next to the Pamir is the Hindu Kush. The Karakoram and Siwalik ranges run alongside each other in Pakistan, India, and Tibet. To the east lie the Transhimalayas and the Lesser Himalayas.

The Himalayas are filled with sheer cliffs, bare rock faces, plunging glaciers, and rushing rivers. They also have the world's highest mountains. More than 60 Himalayan peaks tower above 22,000 feet

(6,700 m). The highest mountain in the world is Mount Everest, at 29,035 feet (8,850 m). The local people call Mount Everest "the Goddess Mother of the World." Annapurna I, at 26,504 feet (8,078 m), is the "Bringer of Life."

Mount Kailas rises near the exact center of the Himalaya Mountains. It is possibly the most sacred mountain in the world. Hindus believe Kailas is a heaven for their gods. Buddhists believe that Kailas is the center of the world.

Five main rivers emerge from Kailas: the Ganges, the Yarlung Tsangpo, the Indus, the Sutlej, and the Karnali. As the Yarlung Tsangpo rushes across India, it becomes known as the Brahmaputra

HOW TALL IS MOUNT EVEREST?

Atlases and encyclopedias list the heights for mountain peaks. Surprisingly, the books may differ on how high a peak is. Two Himalayan mountains, Mount Everest and K2, are the world's tallest. In 1987, two teams of scientists measured the heights of these two peaks using a new instrument called a Global Positioning System, or GPS. One team claimed that K2 stood 29,231 feet (8,909 m) tall and that Everest was 29,195 feet (8,898 m). According to this team, K2 is higher than Everest! The other team declared that Everest rises 29,278 feet (8,924 m), which is higher than K2. Other people who have measured the mountains have come up with different numbers. One book states that Everest is 29,028 feet (8,848 m) tall, while another says it is 29,035 feet (8,850 m). So in reports, it is a good idea to give the source and instrument that was used for geographic measurements.

Snowmelt fills mountain lakes such as Gokyo Lake in Nepal.

River. All these rivers twist and turn through deep mountain valleys on their way to the Indian Ocean.

Most lakes in the Himalayas are frozen. Some, however, such as Rakas, Gokyo, Imja, and Mojang, thaw each spring. They are part of the remarkable Himalayan scenery. Another lake, Mapam Yumco, is considered a holy place. People sometimes pray at Mapam Yumco.

CHAPTER FOUR

PLANTS AND ANIMALS OF THE HIMALAYAS

The Himalayas support a range of plants and wildlife. Tropical birds, animals, and plants fill the lush jungle on the southern slopes. The **temperate** forests of Pakistan and Afghanistan do not have as many vines and trees as tropical forests, but oaks, pines, and

Lush forests paint low-lying Himalayan valleys a deep green.

birches thrive. North of the Himalayas, on the bleak Tibetan **Plateau,** fewer animals and plants survive.

In the tropical forests, chattering monkeys shout from sal trees. A very rare clouded leopard is on the prowl. These cats live only in India, Nepal, and Southeast Asia. They share hunting territory with the dhole, a wild dog. Dholes hunt in packs, preying on wild pigs, deer, sheep, and water buffalo. Tropical forests feature sal trees, cedars, banyans, and pines. Bamboo, a king-sized grass, grows on hills up to 9,900 feet (3,000 m) above sea level. Orchids, ferns, and moss cover much of the forest floor.

Asian black bears, called moon bears, share the forest with tigers and leopards. They are all hunted for their fur. Some hunters ignore laws that protect these animals. They can earn more money from one moon bear skin than from years of farming.

Birds find plenty of food in the Himalayan forests. Red jungle fowl, pheasants, crimson tragopans, and other seed eaters and fruit eaters thrive. Golden eagles and lammergeiers feast on the region's

The monal pheasant, the national bird of Nepal, uses its beak to dig up roots and bulbs.

GRIFFON VULTURES
The griffon vulture is huge. Its wings are 9 feet (3 m) across. The bird's giant wingspan helps it soar effortlessly beside sheer cliffs. Griffons eat dead animal flesh. In the Himalayas, griffon vultures are nature's garbage collectors.

fish, mice, and ground-nesting birds.

In the temperate forests, owls and woodpeckers nest in oaks, pines, cedars, and birches. Musk deer, crowned deer, and sambars graze on dense grasses and wildflowers in forest meadows.

Tundra supports a surprising range of animals and plants. Blue argali sheep, wild goats, yaks, ibex, and takin graze on moss, lichen, and tufts of grass. Marmots and pikas burrow underground to survive the

Yaks are the dairy cattle of the Himalayas. Their milk provides yogurt, butter, and cheese for herd owners.

18

long Himalayan winters.

To the north and east of the Himalayas is the bleak Tibetan Plateau. Although the plateau has a very brutal environment, it hosts the world's largest bears, yaks, and sheep. The Marco Polo sheep grow horns more than 5 feet (1.5 m) long.

The Tibetan Plateau has a brutal climate that few people are willing to endure.

India, Nepal, and Bhutan have established national preserves to save the rare and endangered **species** of the Himalayas. Royal Chitwan in Nepal has thriving populations of Bengal tigers, one-horned rhinoceroses, Asian elephants, and golden monitor lizards. Also in Nepal, Sagamatha National Park protects tahrs, a species of wild goat. In India, Manas Wildlife Sanctuary is home to langurs, tigers, pygmy hogs, Indian rhinoceroses, and Indian elephants.

CHAPTER FIVE

THE PEOPLE OF THE HIMALAYAS

Early humans first arrived in the Himalayas nearly 500,000 years ago. Most likely, they were hunter-gatherers. They hunted large animals for meat. They also collected nuts, berries, fruits, and roots to eat. Some of these people headed north of the Himalayas; others headed south.

Those who headed north moved onto the Tibetan Plateau. They became **nomads,** following large game as the animals searched for grass. Eventually, the people developed into tribes of animal herders.

Many Tibetan people today live much as their relatives did hundreds of years ago. They live in tents called yurts. They live a nomadic life, herding yak. The people have water, shelter, wood for fires, and food. But they do not have indoor plumbing or electricity.

Early people who headed south settled in the Himalayan foothills and valleys. They, too, began as hunter-gatherers. But when

Himalayan farmers grow wheat, millet, rice, and peppers in terraced beds.

large game disappeared, they cleared the land for farming. The

people lived in villages of bamboo or wooden huts.

Today, the descendants of early southern Himalayan people still

farm the land. On the hillsides, they grow rice and other crops such as

peppers, millet, and wheat. The people survive by eating the food they

grow and making whatever goods they need.

Few cities are located in the Himalayas. The region is too remote

for many cities to prosper. The capital cities in Nepal, Tibet, and

Bhutan are the largest in their countries. Kathmandu, Nepal's capital,

is a bustling city of 755,000 people. But Thimphu, the capital of

Bhutan, has only 32,000 people. Rawalpindi and Islamabad, Pakistan, and Srinagar, India, are the largest cities in the Himalayas. They are crowded, busy industrial centers.

Life in a Himalayan city is very different from life in the United States or Canada. Even in the biggest Himalayan cities, many people do not have telephones, televisions, or cars. And in Nepal, only about 12 people in 1,000 have telephones or televisions.

Nepal, Bhutan, and Tibet are among the poorest countries in the world. About four out of ten people live in poverty. The poor of the Himalayas work every day just to eat. There are few doctors, dentists, or hospitals. Poor people in the Himalayas have no way to learn new skills. Parents struggle to survive. Their children will most likely struggle in the same way.

Tibet, which is technically part of China, has seen the most change in the past 20 years. The Chinese government has worked to modernize Tibet. Phone service has improved. Roads, railroads, and electric power plants are updating this ancient region.

There is little industry in the Himalayan countries. Most industry is related to agriculture, such as processing meat and dairy products or making cloth.

Some countries in the Himalayas have mining. Tajikistan mines aluminum, zinc, lead, and chemicals. The

Pedal cabs such as this one in Kathmandu, Nepal, provide transportation at a cheap price.

The best way to tour Royal Chitwan Park is on the back of an elephant.

country produces machine tools, refrigerators, and freezers. Yet six out of ten Tajikistanis live in poverty. Four out of ten cannot find work. The country has 13 television stations, but most people are too poor to afford to buy a television.

A few industries in the Himalayas are growing. Rivers rushing down the Himalayas can be used to create a huge amount of electricity. Electricity created by rushing water is called hydroelectricity. Nepal and Bhutan are building hydroelectric power plants.

Tourism is also on the rise in the Himalayas. Many people come to the Himalayas to climb the peaks, marvel at the scenery, and explore the culture. As tourists flow into the area, so do money and jobs. Tourists need hotels, food, transportation, guides, and other services. Providing these services opens doors to success for Himalayan people.

CHAPTER SIX

THE CULTURE OF THE HIMALAYAS

Most Himalayan people practice one of three religions: Hinduism, Buddhism, or Islam. By far, the most are Hindu and Buddhist. Himalayan festivals and celebrations are usually religious in nature. They involve prayers, feasting, and dancing.

Most Indians and Nepalis are Hindu. Hinduism traces its history back more than 4,000 years. Hindus believe in many gods. The different gods have their own powers and areas of responsibility. Brahma is the creator; Shiva is the destroyer. Hindus believe that they will be reborn after death. A good, respectful life now will lead to a better situation in the next life.

Many Tibetans and Bhutanese are Buddhist. Buddhists follow the teachings of Siddhārtha Gautama—called Buddha. The term *Buddha* means "enlightened one." Buddhists believe in following a path of righteous living, honesty, and decency. By living an honest life, a Buddhist hopes to reach nirvana, a condition in which there is no suffering. Buddhists also believe that after death they are reborn. The cycle of rebirths continues until the Buddhist attains nirvana.

More than 95 percent of Pakistanis and Tajikistanis are Muslim, people who practice Islam. Muslims follow the teachings that the prophet Mohammad established in A.D. 622. Muslims pray five times a day. They must give aid to the poor and follow the laws of the Koran, Islam's holy book.

Pakistani Muslims worship in mosques such as this one in the Hindu Kush.

Eating is central to family life and festivals in the Himalayas. Parents, grandparents, and children dine together. Rice, flat bread, and spices are important to most Himalayan meals. Hindus do not eat beef. Muslims never eat pork. For most people in the Himalayas, meat is eaten only at celebrations.

Indians mix fish, meat, and vegetables with richly spiced curry sauce and

HIMALAYAN TSAMPA
Tsampa is a basic food of the Himalayans. It is roasted ground barley. Tibetans mix tsampa with butter tea to make a meal. Butter tea is a blend of hot water, yak butter, and tea leaves.

put it over rice. They also put a flavorful relish called chutney on their curry. The Bhutanese favor *ema*—spicy chiles in cheese sauce. This hot treat accompanies red or white rice at dinner. Bhutanese eat stews, noodles, and plenty of root vegetables. Nepalese sit down to a plate of rice—*bhat*—with lentil gravy, steamed vegetables, and curry.

At feasts in the Himalayas, musicians play drums and horns. Dancers whirl about in traditional clothing. Many dances date back hundreds of years. They describe the history and culture of people who have long lived high in the magnificent Himalayas.

Glossary

caravans (KA-ruh-vanz) Caravans are long lines of pack animals traveling together. Camel caravans once carried goods across the Hindu Kush.

ecosystems (EE-koh-siss-tuhmz) Ecosystems are communities of plants, animals, water, and soil that work together as a unit and are located in one area. Mountains support a variety of ecosystems.

geologic time (jee-uh-LAH-jik TYME) Geologic time is the long period of time that spans earth's history. The Himalayas were built quickly for geologic time.

glaciers (GLAY-shurz) Glaciers are huge sheets of moving ice. Glaciers cover many Himalayan peaks.

metamorphic (met-uh-MOR-fik) Metamorphic rock is a type of rock formed by high heat and pressure. Gneiss and schist are two types of metamorphic rock.

nomads (NOH-madz) Nomads are people who do not live in one fixed place. Many Tibetans are nomads, moving from place to place following herds of grazing yak.

plateau (pla-TOH) A plateau is a high, flat region. The Tibetan Plateau is a bleak place where few plants and animals survive.

sedimentary (sed-uh-MEN-tuh-ree) Sedimentary rock is formed from the remains of eroded mountains, including sand, clay, rock, salts, and animal remains. Limestone is a type of sedimentary rock.

species (SPEE-sheez) A species is a kind of plant or animal. The snow leopard is an endangered species.

strata (STRAT-uh) Strata are layers of sedimentary rock. If you could look inside a mountain, you could see strata where the rock folded.

temperate (TEM-pur-it) Temperate means mild, such as a temperate climate where it is neither very hot nor very cold. Temperate forests have fewer trees and vines than tropical forests.

tropical (TROP-uh-kuhl) Tropical refers to warm, wet places where temperatures never reach a freezing point. Tropical forests are packed with vines, orchids, and other plants.

tundra (TUHN-druh) Tundra is a treeless ecosystem in the far north or on the upper portion of mountains. Alpine tundra supports fewer animals or plants than forested ecosystems.

A Himalayas Almanac

Extent
    Length: About 1,550 miles (2,500 km)
    Width: About 125 to 250 miles (200 to 400 km)

Continent: Asia

Countries: Afghanistan, Bhutan, India, Nepal, Pakistan, Tajikistan, and Tibet

Major ranges: Hindu Kush, Karakoram, Ladakh, Lesser Himalayas, Pamir, Siwalik, and Transhimalayas

Major rivers: Brahmaputra, Ganges, Indus, Karnali, Sutlej, and Yarlung Tsangpo

Major lakes: Gokyo, Imja, Mapam Yumco, Rakas, and Tilicho

Major cities: Kabul (Afghanistan); Thimphu (Bhutan); Srinagar, (India); Kathmandu (Nepal); Islamabad, Rawalpindi (Pakistan); Lhasa (Tibet)

Major languages: Afghan, Dzongkha, Hindi, Nepali, Pashtu, Punjabi, Tajik, and Tibetan

High Peaks:

Everest	29,035 feet (8,850 m)
K2	28,250 feet (8,611 m)
Kanchenjunga	28,169 feet (8,586 m)
Lhotse	27,923 feet (8,511 m)
Makalu	27,824 feet (8,481m)
Dhaulagiri	26,810 feet (8,172 m)
Manaslu I	26,760 feet (8,156 m)
Cho Oyo	26,750 feet (8,153 m)
Nanga Parbat	26,660 feet (8,126m)
Annapurna I	26,504 feet (8,078 m)

More than 60 peaks over 22,000 feet (6,700 m)

Parks and preserves: Manas Wildlife Sanctuary (Bhutan); Dachigam, Corbett, Manas (India); Royal Chitwan, Sagamatha, Rara, Royal Bardiya (Nepal)

Natural resources: Coal, copper, gold, hydroelectric power, iron ore, mica, and timber

Native birds: Golden eagles, griffon vultures, jungle fowl, lammergeiers, owls, pheasants, tragopans, and woodpeckers

Native mammals: Argali sheep, Asian black bears, Asian elephants, Bengal tigers, clouded leopards, deer, dholes, hares, ibex, langurs, Marco Polo sheep, marmots, mice, monkeys, pikas, pygmy hogs, rhinoceroses, sambars, tahrs, takins, tigers, wild goats, wild pigs, and yaks

Native reptiles: Golden monitor lizards

Native plants: Bamboos, banyans, birches, cedars, ferns, lichens, mosses, oaks, orchids, pines, rhododendrons, and sals

The Himalayas in the News

50 million years ago	The Indian Plate crashes into the Asian Plate, uplifting the Himalayas.
500,000 years ago	Early humans move to the Himalayas.
2000 B.C.	The Hindu religion is founded.
534 B.C.	Siddhartha Gautama begins the religion of Buddhism in India.
622	The prophet Mohammad has the revelations that lead him to found Islam.
1271–1275	Italian trader Marco Polo travels to China through the Himalayas.
1852	Mount Everest is measured and found to be the tallest mountain on earth.
1907	Bhutan becomes a Buddhist monarchy.
1910	Tibet gets its first postal service.
1947	India becomes independent from Great Britain.
1951	China assumes control of Tibet.
1953	Edmund Hillary and Tenzing Norgay become the first people to climb Mount Everest.
1973	Royal Chitwan becomes the first national park in Nepal.
1991	Tajikistan gains independence from the Soviet Union.
2003	Heavy flooding occurs along the Ganges River.

How to Learn More about the Himalayas

At The Library

NONFICTION

Chester, Jonathan. *Young Adventurer's Guide to Everest: From Avalanche to Zopkiok.* Berkeley, Calif.: Tricycle Press, 2002.

Cooper, Robert. *Bhutan.* Tarrytown, N.Y.: Benchmark Books, 2001.

Sis, Peter. *Tibet: Through the Red Box.* New York: Farrar Straus & Giroux, 1998.

Venables, Stephen. *To the Top: The Story of Everest.* Cambridge, Mass.: Candlewick Press, 2003.

FICTION

Rankin, Louise. *Daughter of the Mountains.* New York: Puffin Press, 1993.

Whitesel, Cheryl Aylward. *Rebel: A Tibetan Odyssey.* New York: William Morrow, 2000.

On the Web

VISIT OUR HOME PAGE FOR LOTS OF LINKS ABOUT THE HIMALAYAS:

http://www.childsworld.com/links.html

Note to Parents, Teachers, and Librarians: We routinely verify our Web links to make sure they're safe, active sites—so encourage your readers to check them out!

Places to Visit or Contact

DEPARTMENT OF TOURISM
PO Box 126
Thimphu, Bhutan
www.tourism.gov.bt

NEPAL TOURISM BOARD
Bhrikuti Mandap
Kathmandu, Nepal
www.welcomenepal.com

TIBET HOUSE
22 West 15th Street
New York, NY 10011
212/807-0563
www.tibethouse.org

Index

About the Author

Barbara A. Somervill is the author of many books for children. She loves learning and sees every writing project as a chance to learn new information or gain a new understanding. Somervill grew up in New York State, but she has also lived in Toronto, Canada; Canberra, Australia; California; and South Carolina. She currently lives with her husband in Simpsonville, South Carolina.